What is Recycling?

Recycling is the process of making things from materials that have already been used.

Common and not so common

The most common materials recycled are paper, aluminium, plastic and glass, but many everyday items can also be recycled, such as printer cartridges, car batteries and mobile phones.

Whether or not something is recycled often depends on the cost. Aluminium is recycled because it is inexpensive to turn into new aluminium products, and because making new aluminium is expensive. Steel is much cheaper to produce from raw materials, so there is less incentive to recycle it – although it can be recycled easily.

Everyday recycling

Everyday household waste is recycled. This reduces the amount of rubbish that goes into dumps and landfills.

Organic matter, such as food scraps, is turned into compost for the garden. Newspapers, glass bottles, aluminium cans and plastic containers are separated from the rest of the rubbish. They are then collected usually by your local council, and sent to companies that specialise in sorting and reprocessing materials for recycling.

A way of thinking

There will probably always be materials that cannot be recycled and will become rubbish. However, recycling is part of an overall approach to using the Earth's resources wisely. It encourages using fewer materials and reusing materials many times before recycling them or throwing them away.

Recycling cars is one of the oldest forms of recycling. Using recycled car parts can halve the cost of some car repair jobs.

More than 90 per cent of the materials in mobile phones can be recycled to make new products, like batteries, jewellery, toys and fence posts.

GO FACT!

DID YOU KNOW?

One kilogram of gold can be recovered from the circuits of about 50 000 mobile phones.

Most new car batteries contain parts from recycled batteries.

Waste bricks can be crushed and used to make driveways, or sold to a brick recycler.

5

Why Recycle?

Recycling helps to conserve the Earth's natural resources and reduces pollution and the amount of energy we use.

Natural resources

There is a limit to the amount of oil in the Earth from which we can make plastic, and a limit to the amount of aluminium **ore** to make cans. Resources that will run out eventually are called **finite resources**. Recycling reduces our consumption of finite resources.

Also, when recycled materials are used to make new products, they don't go into dumps or landfills, so land is conserved.

Energy

Making products from recycled materials often uses much less energy than producing the same products from raw materials. Less energy consumed means less of the **greenhouse gases**, such as carbon dioxide and methane, is created. This helps prevent **global warming**.

Recycling just one plastic bottle can save the amount of energy needed to run a light bulb for six hours.

Pollution

In most cases, recycling materials creates less air and water pollution than making products from materials that have not been previously used.

Recycling our waste also means less burning of rubbish, which causes air pollution, and less rubbish rotting in dumps, which produces methane.

DID YOU KNOW?

On average, each person in the UK throws away seven times their body weight in rubbish every year.

Each household produces about one tonne of rubbish annually, amounting to about 27 million tonnes for the UK each year.

At least half the contents of our dustbins could be recycled, but only 12 per cent is actually recycled or composted.

It can take more than three litres of oil to make one printer cartridge.

85 per cent of litter is made up of packaging waste. Most of this could be recycled.

Types of Waste

CORROSIVES

Homes and industries produce **biodegradable**, non-biodegradable and **hazardous** waste.

Decomposing naturally

Biodegradable waste is anything that **decomposes** naturally. **Micro-organisms** break down the waste into water, carbon dioxide and minerals, which nourish plants and improve soil quality. Most organic materials, such as food scraps and paper, are biodegradable. Some types of plastic made from plants are also biodegradable.

If biodegradable waste is buried in landfills with other types of waste, it does not have the oxygen, light and water it requires to decompose.

Here for a long time

Non-biodegradable waste does not break down naturally and must be recycled, burnt or buried.

A common non-biodegradable product is the plastic shopping bag. Plastic bags take anywhere between 15 and 1000 years to break down in the environment. Every year, they kill at least 100 000 birds, whales, seals and turtles that choke on the bags or become trapped in them.

Shops and governments are trying to reduce the use of bags by either charging shoppers for each bag they use or banning them altogether.

Handle carefully

Waste that burns or explodes, or is **toxic** to people or the environment, is known as hazardous waste. It is usually the by-product of industrial processes, but common household products used for cleaning and gardening are also hazardous when thrown away.

Like non-biodegradable waste, some hazardous wastes can be recycled. For example, engine oils can be cleaned and reused, or burnt to provide energy.

DID YOU KNOW?

Here's how long it takes some products to biodegrade if they are dropped as litter.

Paper	2–5 months
Rope	3–14 months
Orange peel	6 months
Cigarette butt	1–12 years
Plastic-coated paper milk carton	5 years
Nylon fabric	30–40 years
Tin can	50–100 years
Aluminium can	80–100 years
Plastic 6-pack holder rings	450 years
Glass bottle	1 million years

Sorting types of waste is an important part of the recycling process.

Since 2002, Ireland has reduced its use of supermarket plastic bags by 90 per cent.

Dumps

Rubbish dumps are large, open areas of rubbish. They are not designed to process waste – they simply get bigger as people dump more rubbish.

Health hazards

All kinds of waste – including hazardous waste and recyclable materials – are left uncovered on a dump. When it rains, water seeps down through the rubbish and becomes **contaminated**. This water is called **leachate**. It is an environmental and health hazard because it can flow into rivers and lakes, and **ground water** below the dump.

Dumps attract insects, rats, birds and other **scavenging** animals, which can spread disease. Rubbish is burnt at some dumps, producing harmful air pollution. The wind carries pollution and the bad smell of the dump to where people live.

Fires out of control

Rubbish dumps are also fire hazards. A large dump can start burning by itself due to the heat produced by rotting materials. It is difficult for firefighters to get under the rubbish to the source of these fires which are often left to burn.

Some people live in rubbish dumps and rely on the daily dumping of waste for food and items they can sell.

n the UK there are special rules bout the disposal of fridges and eezers to protect the environment.

Leachate carries pollution from whatever has been dumped.

GO FACT!

DID YOU KNOW?

The first rubbish dump was created in 500 BC by the ancient Greeks in Athens. Rubbish had to be dumped at least 1.5 kilometres away from the city's wall.

In 2000 an avalanche at the Payatas dump in Manila, Philippines, killed more than 300 people who were trying to make a living scavenging off the dump.

Landfills

Landfills are built to bury rubbish. They are like sealed containers, separating rubbish from air and water.

What goes in

A landfill is lined with a thick layer of **clay** or plastic to stop the rubbish and leachate leaking out. The landfill site is divided into sections or cells. Rubbish is crushed and **compacted**, and any liquid is drained away, before it is tipped into a cell.

At the end of each day, the cell is covered with a thick layer of soil to minimise the smell and keep pests away.

What comes out

Landfills are kept as dry as possible to stop leachate from seeping into the soil underneath the landfill. A network of drains at the bottom of the landfill collects the leachate. A treatment plant can then extract clean water from it.

Landfills also produce gases, mainly methane and carbon dioxide, from the decomposing rubbish.

Playing on rubbish

When a landfill is full, it is closed by covering it with a thick layer of soil, and grass is planted to stop the soil from eroding. The site – especially the ground water – is then monitored for gas and leachate production for up to 30 years.

Some time after a landfill is closed, the ground may be used for parks, golf courses or sporting fields.

Landfills can become sports fields.

The amount of landfill waste produced by the UK every two hours is enough to fill the Albert Hall in London.

Rubbish decomposes slowly in landfills — when old landfills have been dug up, 40-year-old newspapers that can still be read have been found.

GO FACT!

DID YOU KNOW?

Every year the world throws away 1.2 billion tyres. Rather than dumping them, they could be recycled into oil and steel, and rubber to make roads, walls, pipes and floor tiles.

Paper takes up as much as 50 per cent of landfill space.

Compost

Compost is a loose, dirt-like substance made by the natural breakdown of organic material by micro-organisms. Composting can recycle lots of kitchen and garden waste.

Natural decay

In forests, compost is formed from leaves and fruit that fall to the ground. As these decay, their **nutrients** are absorbed by the soil and feed the forest.

Composting at home is the same process, only faster. It can be done on an open heap or in an enclosure or bin, which keeps the rain and pests out.

Ingredients of compost

The essential requirements of composting are nutrients, micro-organisms, air, water and time.

Nutrients come from the carbon in leaves, plant cuttings and newspaper, and the nitrogen in grass cuttings, fruit and vegetable scraps. Soil adds the micro-organisms needed to break down the nutrients.

Water and air allow the micro-organisms to continue to breed. They produce carbon dioxide and heat, and the compost must be turned with a garden fork so that heat and air circulate through the heap.

If the decay process works well in the heap, compost is produced in about 8–10 weeks.

The temperature inside a compost heap can reach 70 °C.

Double recycling! Many compost bins are made out of recycled plastic.

IN YOUR COMPOST HEAP

What to add	What NOT to add
Leaves	Meat and dairy products
Vegetable and food scraps	Fat
Soft stems	Metals, plastic, glass
Used vegetable cooking oil	Cat and dog droppings
Wet newspapers	Magazines
Grass cuttings	Large branches
Coffee grounds	Bones
Tea-leaves and tea bags	Weeds with seeds

Recycling Aluminium

Aluminium is used to make drink cans, cars, planes and building materials. It is recycled because it is cheaper to recycle than to make from raw materials.

Metal from the ground

Aluminium is made from the mineral ore alumina, found in bauxite. Most bauxite mining is in the Caribbean, Australia and Africa. In a process called smelting, a strong electrical current is passed through **liquefied** alumina to separate aluminium metal.

The aluminium is melted in a furnace and poured into moulds to make aluminium ingots. To make drink cans, the ingots are rolled into sheets 2.5 millimetres thick.

Aluminium scooters

Melted

Aluminium is easy to recycle. Cans collected from recycling centres are crushed and compacted into bales. They are then melted in a furnace at 700 °C, and again poured into moulds to make ingots. Aluminium can be recycled ove and over, without adding new materials.

Saving energy

Recycling saves 95 per cent of the energy it would take to mal new aluminium from raw materials. This is because two stages which use a lot of energ are left out – mining the bauxit and extracting the alumina.

Using less energy means fewer greenhouse gases are released into the atmosphere.

A bale of aluminium cans weighs 7–15 kilograms. Recycling one aluminium can saves enough electricity to run a television for three hours.

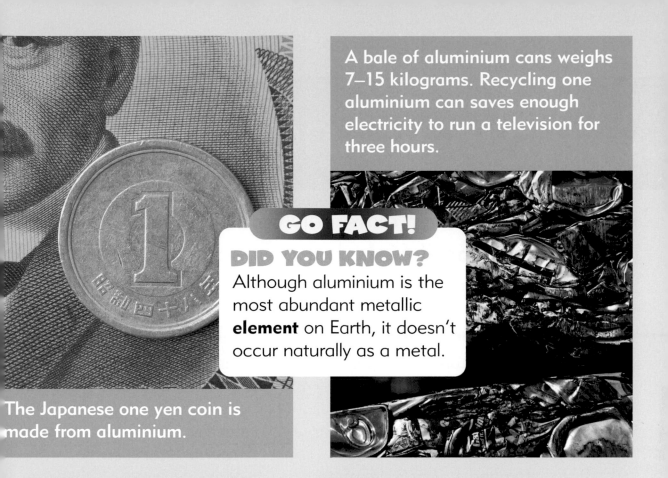

GO FACT!

DID YOU KNOW?
Although aluminium is the most abundant metallic **element** on Earth, it doesn't occur naturally as a metal.

The Japanese one yen coin is made from aluminium.

Aluminium **alloys** are used to make aircraft because of their light weight and strength.

Aluminium transfers heat rapidly and can be made into thin sheets, so drinks in aluminium cans can chill very quickly.

Recycling Plastic

Plastic is an extremely **versatile** material made from **fossil fuels**, but only some types of plastic are regularly recycled.

Identifying types

Manufacturers stamp a code on plastic products to identify different types. This code is a number inside the triangular recycling arrows. Plastics stamped 1, 2 or 3 are often recycled, while plastics stamped 4, 5, 6 or 7 usually are not.

Some plastics made from plants, such as corn, are biodegradable. They can be composted and returned to the soil. McDonald's has used biodegradable cutlery at its restaurants in Austria and Sweden.

PET recycling

Plastic stamped with identification code 1 are PET (polyethylene terephthalate) plastics, often used as soft drir water and juice bottles.

PET bottles are recycled by separating them from other ty of plastic, and sorting them in different colour groups: clear, blue and green, and a mixed colour group.

They are then crushed and transported to the recycler.

Once there, they are sorted ag washed and then shredded into flakes. The flakes are washed, dried and melted to make new plastic products: fleece clothin pillows, carpets, rope, sleeping bags, life jackets, furniture, building materials – and more PET bottles.

It takes 25 two-litre PET bottles to make one fleece jacket.

The labels on PET bottles are removed during recycling, but always remember to remove the lids before putting bottles in your recycling bin.

It takes 125 plastic milk bottles to make one 140-litre wheelie bin.

GO FACT!

DID YOU KNOW?

80 million tonnes of plastic are produced each year, using up to eight per cent of the world's oil production.

Recycling Glass

Glass is one of the best materials to recycle – it can be recycled over and over again.

The importance of sorting

Glass for recycling is sorted by colour: clear, amber and green. Materials that contaminate the glass, such as metal bottle tops, crockery and pieces of mirror, are removed. As little as five grams of ceramic material – such as a piece of crockery the size of a fingernail – in a tonne of glass is enough to mean the glass must be sorted again or sent to landfill.

Making cullet

The glass is crushed into **culle** Cullet is often mixed with the r materials of glass (sand, soda ash and limestone) before beir melted in a furnace at up to 1500° Celsius.

The molten glass is poured int moulding machines and air is blown through it to shape new glass products. These are coo down slowly before they can b used.

Recycling glass saves space ir landfills, and because recyclec glass melts at a lower temperature than raw materia it saves energy. The energy saved from recycling one glas: bottle is enough to power a lig bulb for four hours.

Sorting waste glass by colour is an important part of the recycling process, so that glass of one colour is made into new products of the same colour.

Pieces of glass that are too small to be recycled into glass bottles can be made into very fine granules. The granules don't have sharp edges and are used to make concrete and tiles, and can even be used instead of sand in sand pits.

Glass
• Separate by color / Remove Lids.
• Keep Breakage to minimum.
• Container Glass only.
(No Window Glass, Please.)

Brown Glass   Green Glass   Clear Glass

GO FACT!

DID YOU KNOW?

Switzerland recycles 91 per cent of its glass – the highest rate in the world. The UK recycles approximately 46 per cent of its glass.

Recycling Paper

Recycling paper conserves water and trees, and saves room in landfills.

Most but not all

Most paper can be recycled, but government and company files, and paper in books, are usually not available for recycling. Paper in plasterboard, a building material, can't be recycled and nor can tissues or wax paper.

Making pulp

Paper is made by mixing wood chips with water to separate the wood fibres. This mixture is called **pulp**. The pulp is rolled over mesh and flattened to remove the water, then cut into sheets and dried.

Recycled paper is made in the same way, but with used paper instead of wood chips. Paper for recycling is sorted into cardboard, newspaper, office paper and liquid paperboard (juice and milk containers). It is shredded and mixed with water to make pulp.

It takes much less water to make pulp from recycled paper than from wood chips.

New products

Newspaper and office paper are recycled into **newsprint**, cardboard and notebooks. Recycled cardboard is used to make more cardboard products such as egg cartons and toilet roll tubes. Milk and juice cartons made from liquid paperboard, are made into high-quality office paper.

Greeting cards are recycled as packaging and toilet paper.

It takes just one hour to make a new recycled paper roll that is 14 kilometres long.

Every time paper is recycled, its fibres become weaker, which limits the number of times it can be recycled. Paper can usually be recycled eight times.

Make Your Own Paper

Make your own recycled paper from old newspapers.

Each sheet of paper will take a couple of days to dry. When making other sheets, try adding pieces of coloured paper to the bucket of newspaper pieces, or **embed** a leaf in the sheet by placing it on top of the pulp that you spread across the screen.

You will need:

- newspaper
- bucket
- warm water
- wooden board
- cup
- blender
- piece of flyscreen (polyester mesh) attached to a frame
- extra frame – same size with no mesh
- large plastic tub
- large cloth.

1 Tear the newspaper into small pieces. Place them in the bucket, cover with water and soak for an hour.

2 Place one cup of the wet paper mixture and two cups of warm water in the blender (ask an adult to help with the blender). If it does not blend easily, add more water. This mixture is the pulp.

3 Pour the pulp into the tub. Add three litres of water. Place the two frames together with the empty frame on top of the mesh. Hold together with a hand on each side.

4 Lower the frame into the tub, screen side up. Lift the frames out of the tub, keeping them horizontal. Let the water drain away.

5 Lift the empty frame off carefully. Cover the board with wet cloth. Tip your paper onto the wet cloth, pushing down firmly. Lift off the screen. You can now make another sheet of paper.

25

Energy from Waste

Waste that is not recycled can be turned into energy. This reduces our use of non-renewable energy sources like oil and natural gas.

Rotting organic matter

As organic matter in landfills breaks down it produces landfill gas, usually a mixture of carbon dioxide and methane gas. Landfill gas can be used as a fuel instead of coal or gas in power plants. This prevents methane escaping into the atmosphere, which is important because it is a more **potent** greenhouse gas than carbon dioxide.

Fuel from plants

Landfill gas is a **biomass fuel** – a fuel from plant material or agricultural waste. Other biomass fuels are sewage gas, rice husks and bagasse, the sugar cane waste from the sugar refining industry.

Biomass fuels are renewable energy sources because plants use the renewable resources water, carbon dioxide and sunlight to grow. So, although burning them still releases greenhouse gases into the atmosphere, they reduce the use of non-renewable fuels.

Choosing 'green'

You can choose to have electricity generated from renewable sources, such as biomass fuels, supplied to your home. This is called 'green energy'. Although it costs a little more, buying green energy is a great way to encourage the development of a power industry that doesn't rely only on non-renewable fossil fuels.

sugar cane

Biomass fuels don't have to come from waste — some grasses and trees, such as willows and these poplars, are grown especially to generate energy.

The ash left over from burning bagasse can be used as a soil conditioner or added to fertiliser on cane farms.

Methane, a by-product of industry, is sometimes just burnt in flares rather than used to generate electricity.

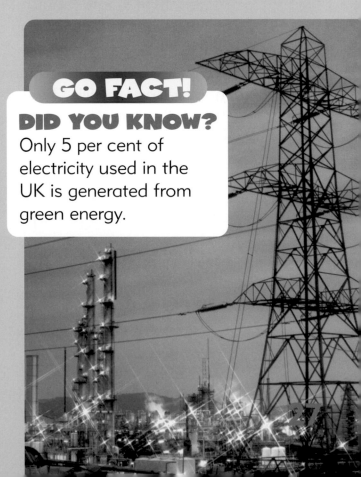

GO FACT!

DID YOU KNOW?

Only 5 per cent of electricity used in the UK is generated from green energy.

Should We Always Recycle

Recycling saves energy and natural resources and reduces the production of greenhouse gases. But it can be expensive and is not possible for all types of waste.

Saving money

Recycling saves money because there are lower manufacturing costs for products made from recycled rather than new materials. It keeps rubbish out of landfills, which saves the cost of landfill dumping fees and reduces the cost of building and maintaining landfills. There is also the value of saved natural resources.

Some people make money from recycling. Companies collect and sell materials to recycle, and new recycling technologies are developed and sold.

Spending money

Recycling also costs money. There is a cost to collect, transport and process recyclable materials, and the trucks that transport materials use fossil fuels and pollute the air. Recycling centres must be built and operated.

Some items are expensive to recycle, especially if there is no a large quantity to recycle. If th recycled material is not sold, th recycler will not make money.

Towards zero

Recycling is not a complete solution to handling waste. The real solution is to reduce our us of packaging and products. So what is better than recycling? Zero waste! The goal of zero waste is to design products tha are made to be reused, repaire recycled or composted – to minimise and ultimately eliminate waste.

Need a new computer? Don't dump your old one! Instead, you could:

- donate your working computer to a refurbishing centre where it can be resold
- give it to someone else, or a school or charity
- take your computer to a recycling centre.

Most parts of a computer can be saved from going into a landfill. The components can be removed and sold, or the metals, glass and plastics stripped out for recycling.

GO FACT!

DID YOU KNOW?
There are 10 million mobile phones that could be recycled stored in UK homes.

The next time you are in a supermarket, notice how things are packaged.

Some UK supermarkets now sell reusable bags for using for your shopping.

29

Turning Plastic into ...

Plastic code	Originally made into ...	Can be recycled as ...
1	drink bottles, pillow filling, clothing	drink bottles, clear packaging, film, carpet, fleece clothing
2	crinkly shopping bags, freezer bags, shampoo bottles, milk bottles, milk crates	compost and recycling bins, rubbish bins, flower pots, detergent bottles, agricultural pipes
3	clear juice bottles, plumbing pipes, garden hoses, bags to hold blood	detergent bottles, hoses, floor coverings, plumbing pipes
4	rubbish bags, ice-cream container lids, squeezy bottles, rubbish bins	concrete lining, rubbish bags, shopping bags
5	crisp packets, ice-cream containers, drinking straws, lunch boxes	compost bins, recycling crates
6	yoghurt containers, plastic cutlery, takeaway food containers, meat trays	clothes pegs, coat hangers, office accessories
7	lids and assorted containers	computer and telephone cases, agricultural pipes